A Drifter's
ATLAS

A Drifter's Atlas
Copyright © 2018 by Cheyenne Reid.

All rights reserved. No part of this publication may be reproduced, distributed, or transmitted in any form or by any means, including photocopying, recording, or other electronic or mechanical methods, without the prior written permission of the copyright holder, except in the case of brief quotations embodied in critical reviews and certain other noncommercial uses permitted by copyright law. For permission requests, write to the publisher, addressed "Attention: Permissions Coordinator," at the address below.

ISBN: 978-1-64318-014-4

Book cover design by Mary Des.
Interior layout design by Kristen Polson.

Imperium Publishing
1097 N. 400th Rd
Baldwin City, KS, 66006

www.imperiumpublishing.com

A Drifter's ATLAS

FINDING THE PEACE IN SOLITUDE

POETRY BY

Cheyenne Reid

I dedicate this to the drifters. The dreamers. The strayers. The vagabonds.
The broken-hearted, the heart-breakers, and the ones with newfound love.
To the ones who have restless souls
and a never-ending desire to discover who they truly are.

I encourage you to keep your wander, find yourself,
and get lost in this beautiful life.

The contents within these bindings are filled with the constant struggles between the mind and heart. It is compiled with the ups and downs that come with life. This atlas has its roadblocks, its detours. It has winding hills and wide open spaces. There are setbacks, and there is freedom. We may never know what lies ahead, as well as we may never know what emotions each day will bring. As you're reading, you will notice that *A Drifter's Atlas* is meant to represent these moments.

I've always heard there is peace in solitude
But I've never tested that theory
Until now

And I've found there is peace
Eventually

After a heartbreak
After the constant emptiness as you're alone
For the first time in what feels like centuries

After the numbness you've adapted to
As you searched for companionship
In strangers' beds

Just to realize that they too
Are just as numb as you

You'll discover it
When you're left with no one but yourself
And you're forced to ask
"Who am I really?"

That is when it comes in like a tidal wave, Darling

So, who are you?

You are the force of a thousand storms

Do not settle for anyone
Who thinks anything less of you

The sad truth is, my dear,
In my mind

I'm already gone.

You used to be the head rush I'd get
When I picked you up for the first time

You were the chills that crawled down my spine
With just a single touch

I used to be fascinated
By the smoke rolling off my lips
After I breathed you in so deeply

But I realize now
The smoke fades
And the chills cease

And after a while
You became
Just something to do with my hands

I made a habit out of you

I have lost my mind
trying to understand yours

Or maybe
It was already gone
If I ever thought I could

With trembling hands
We are all out here

Just trying to be Brave

Damn you.

For making my only memories
I took away from us
Be the ones of you telling me
All the things I did wrong

Damn you.

For completely shattering me
Just so you could rebuild me into
Whoever you wanted me to be

Thank you.

If it wasn't for you
I wouldn't have been able
To pick up the pieces of myself
That I didn't know I had been missing

Thank you.

For being the fuel to this fire
That I forgot I had

Now watch me burn your world down

No one should feel like they have to
Bare the weight of their emotions
For the sake of not inconveniencing others

                              You are not a burden.

There is something beautiful
About people
Who have felt heartbreak
But remain unbroken

They love harder than the rest

All I needed was for you to
Tell me this is what's best for us
Tell me that this is okay

But you didn't
And feelings have changed

And now neither of us
Can get dressed fast enough

Now I can't ask you to
Please don't go
Because even I don't want to stay

And now I can't help but wonder
Who fell out of love first

For I've filled my soul with so much fire
That no one can get close enough

Without getting burnt.

When he asked me
For my forever

Why did it feel
As if he was asking
To clip my wings?

I've never been ordinary
    So what makes you think
        That I'll settle for such?

I gave my all to you
Without hesitation
For nothing in return

        Is this my fucked-up version of love?

All I've ever wanted
Was to be your Muse

        Now I'm left trying to make sense of
        the remaining fragments of myself
        That you had no use for

And this I hope you know
    That one day

                    Your aching soul
                      Will find a home again.

I will never be ashamed of being a good lover
The one thing I do regret, though,
Is being one
To the wrong person

I have the tendency to give
All of myself to the ones I love
Without hesitation

Just to be disappointed
When I need them
And no one shows up

And then they wonder why
I'm always on the run
Why I prefer to be alone

For I know what I have to offer
And I now realize that
I have to become who I've always needed
I need to be enough for me

They've always called you
The life of the party

They've always said
You brighten any room you walk in

But what they don't see
Is the empty spaces where you escape
To release your demons

So that others don't have to know you suffer

My Love, you're always saving everyone else
As you're drowning in your own self-doubt

I think it's time
For you to swim to the top
And gasp for fresh air

I used up all of my matches
Trying to make our fire burn again

To be able to think of them
And feel nothing

But the faint memory
Of someone that you used to know

That's how you'll know the pain is over

Head filled with already broken promises
As soon as the words escape your lips

You'd think that after all of the lies you've told
I'd be immune to the pain they inflict

                         They still sting just the same.

I do not regret what we had
Because of you

I was forced to find comfort
In myself

—You were never there.

So I'll go quietly
Slip into the haze of the unknown,

For that seems more inviting
Than your arms now-a-days

I know what it is like
To have a trusting heart

And to have it completely dismantled

Do not let that be the foundation
For unbreakable walls

        Protect it
        But don't make it impossible
        To let love in

I gave you my all
And all that I wasn't
To try to appease whatever fucked-up fantasy
Of a lover you concocted at the time

Just to find out
That I still was not good enough
No matter what mold I forced myself into

I don't know what hurts worse:

Being walked away from
Or walking away from someone you love

In order to save yourself

You begged me to stay
Tears rolled down your face

And with all of my heart
I wanted to feel something,
Anything at all

I wanted to want you
But honey,
You can only push someone
Away for so long

Until they drift too far
To hear your cry

"So I guess I'll see you
When I see you,"

I said
As I stood in the doorway

We should have known it would
End this way

I had always wanted to
Fall off the map

When you had only
Wanted me to fall
For you

I'm sorry

But I was not strong enough
To save us both.

I had to let go

So I packed up my suitcase
Filled it with useless shit and my tethered heart
And ran as fast
And as far away from you
As I possibly could

—Coast to Coast

Because you,
You are Strong

Our blood does not cower
We face challenges head on
And headstrong

With love in our hearts
And empathy for the unknown

I know my faults

I know my communication
Could be better

I know I shut down
When I'm hurt

I am aware that I get lost in my mind
More frequently than not

That I find comfort in writing
Rather than you

I don't mean to hide from you

I just haven't experienced
Someone who cares quite like you do

I have realized that I am terrified of commitment
 It seems as if my heart desires to love
but when love comes around
I hesitate
Where did I go wrong?

Do I crave independence so much
That I can't imagine leaning on someone?

Not now, anyway, for I am too far gone

And after so many years,
The moment he begged me to stay

Was the first time he dropped to his knees
And worshiped the fucking Goddess
That I've always been

I tend to get lost within the pines
In order to find myself
The wilderness has become
My beautiful escape

Time is fleeting
As is my heart

And it seems as if
No one can catch up to either

For I do not know what tomorrow holds
Or if it will even accept me

So I shall continue to live each day

    With a grateful heart,
        An open mind,
                And eyes wide open

I became so fixed on
becoming detached from
any city and any man

that I believe I may have forgotten
how to tie knots

So I left
And it wasn't because you didn't care enough
Maybe it was that you cared too much

That I felt like no matter what I did
You'd still love me this hard
You'd still want me this much

You gave me your heart
Cut the strings and forfeited it over
While I kept mine in hand
Locked to my chest
Always on guard

I just didn't know how to give it away as you do

I just don't know if I know how to love that hard

You deserve someone who can
Someone who will
So I Left

Did you forget who you are?

        Surely you don't think
        That this is all you are capable of

         For you were made
        To not only conquer mountains

        But to crush them

She stands in front of a mirror
Wearing nothing but a smile

She notes every little scar and mark
As a sign of past battles won

She gently runs her hands
Around her soft curves

Without hesitation

There is nothing quite as powerful

As a Woman
Who accepts every part of who she is

I've found that leaving
Is what I'm best at

As if I'm addicted to goodbyes

Maybe I feel as if people get too close;
That I'm too exposed

So I shall continue to drift
Until I find someone

Who makes my desire to stay
Stronger than my urge to run

Gazing out the window
At the city lights below
Mimicking stars above

And though they may be brighter
They just can't quite shine the same

—Flying over San Francisco

"Where are you off to now?"
You ask, sitting up against the headboard
As I slip my shirt back on

"Anywhere but here," says my mind
As my lips kiss you goodbye

Her heart was like an ocean

So vast and
filled with undiscovered spaces

That hid a treasure
Every pirate searched for

While she had only been waiting
For a Sailor
Who could handle the raging waves
Of her soul

To be honest
Letting go of you
Felt like taking that first breath
After drowning

My biggest fear

Is waking up one day

With wrinkled hands
Brittle bones

And dreams that I failed
To make into my reality

So let's go make some memories
To tell our kids
And our kids' kids
About the
Crazy
Adventurous
Lives we led

So maybe they too
Will choose to
See it
And
Feel it
All
For what it is

We settle on the idea
That we must work
Our lives away
To stay in debt
to materialistic things

Don't you see?
Not only is your wallet suffering
But also, is your soul

There are times that
I wish for an average life

That sometimes it may be easier
Than the challenges I face now

But then I meet a stranger
Who is filled with wisdom

Or witness a sunset
That brings tears
To the eyes

And it makes me realize
How damn beautiful
This life is

That there is much more out there
Than average

Show me the colors
Of a world
Other than my own

For mine are getting a little dull

Under this flesh
And aching bones
And hollow heart

Lies a soul
That's only desire
Is to be found

There are times
When you need to know
That you are not invincible

That you too
Are human
Just as those around you

To be brought down to Earth
And respect another's journey
As if it is your own

How can someone accept me
When I can't even accept myself?

You say you don't amount to much
I watch you tear yourself apart
While I can only be a voice in the background
Telling you you're wrong

I wish you could see you through my eyes

The way you enter a room and the whole crowd stops to look at you
Or how your smile and laughter could instantly fix my worst day

If you could feel the immediate comfort I find the moment I'm in your arms
Or my heart when our gazes meet across a filled room

You say you don't amount to much
But baby
You've quickly become
More than enough to me

You laughed so freely
That it bound me in shackles

To you

Feeling the warmth of the sun
Stinging your skin

And the rumbling roar
Of an engine

And the wind sweeping
Your hair

And the music
Filling the air

That
To me
Is freedom

You expose your demons to me
While we lie in our hotel bed
Intoxicated on whiskey
And each other

You tell me of your past
The depression and anxiety

The way you felt moments before
You wanted to end it all

I bury my face into your chest
My heart is pierced by the thought
The possibility that we could've not
Been where we are right now
Together

All I can say is "baby…"
And hold back the tears
And hide the cracking emotion in my voice

To think of you in that state
Alone
Afraid
Confused

I've never felt my heartbreak that way before
Never felt someone so real yet a dream to me

You expose your demons to me
And in that I know
I would spend all my days
Driving them away
If you'd let me

"You've made your bed," you said.
"Now you have to lay in it."

When darling, all I want is to make a mess of yours.

Did they wake up this morning, and brew a cup of coffee
Or get ready while listening to their favorite song?

Did they make breakfast beside the one they love most
Or was this their first morning waking up alone?

We never wonder enough about other people
We see them for who they are in this very moment,
Judging the value of a human being as if its equivalent to the price tag
of the fabrics that cover their naked bodies

Or the expressions they are wearing
Like it's a representation of their soul

We forget that they are out here trying to survive
Just like you and I

Too many try
To change the tide

Whenever we are meant
To ride the waves

CHEYENNE REID

As I grab my bags
And drift along

City after city

The thought of coming home
To you one day
Is gentle on my mind

Sugar,
Let's live a life

That keeps us young

Your lips
My whiskey

Your laughter
My drug

Your soul
My Vice

I don't believe I've felt an addiction
Quite like this

We lie there
Hiding from the morning sun
Tangled up with you
In yet another hotel bed
Another city
Just passing through

"I think I love you most in the morning"
You whisper to me
With your sleepy eyes locked on mine
As you run your fingers through my hair

                                      and just like that, I come undone.

It is not you, My Love
For I was made to roam

So I will carry your heart with me
And I shall return it to you someday

For my bones have found a place to rest now
With you

My walls effortlessly fall to the ground
like leaves when autumn turns to cold

                    I am
                    Exposed,
                    Unraveled,
                    And helplessly in love

Venturing out into an unfamiliar city
Filled with all things new

She weaves through the crowds
With her head in the clouds

Her desires are simple;
To be amongst a sea of faces
Who do not recognize hers

And to feed her undeniable craving
For the unknown

Death is not something you can escape
It will come knocking on your door
sooner
or later

And I hope you choose to live your days
With an ungodly amount of
love
and wander

Let your soul be free, my Dear
While it's still yours

— you think you have time.

To see the world
My Dear
Is to see life
As we know it

Why should we waste our younger years

Just to be free to roam
When we lose our youthful
Sense of wander?

It is a trap way too many fall into

I woke up to the sound of waves crashing into each other outside of my balcony door. I had left it open throughout the night, and the smell of saltwater inhabited the hotel room as I laid tangled up in the white sheets. The sun was just barely touching my side of the Earth, so I forced myself out of the bed and ran down to the beach to answer the wave's call. It was like the ocean knew I needed to witness this morning's sunrise...

There are a lot of things in this life that are hard. There are obstacles every day that each soul has to overcome, and it is so easy to dwell on the difficult. But I feel like we need less of this. We need less of what this materialistic society demands we give them. We need less of the unnecessary drama in the news. We need less consumption. Less worry. We need more laughter. More encouragement. More love for the land we all share. We need more simplicity. And we damn sure need a lot more sunrises.

I encourage you to do something that helps you, that brings you down to Earth. Go outside and feel the warmth from the sun kiss your skin. Get a little dirty. Love one another. Respect everyone's journey. Let's stop dwelling in the difficult and start living in the now.

Grey skies
Don't always fade

Sometimes you have to learn
To find peace with the rain

For removing myself
From my comfort zone

Has given me so much life
That even my dreams
Are envious

The problem is
We treat others
As if the world is our own
And anyone else
is just the bystander
In our story

It is about time
We start living in third person

Lying here with only the memory
of who you used to be

My version of sleeping with a stranger

If only we cared
About the Earth around us
Half as much as we care about
the virtual world we have created
My darling, it would be evergreen

Sparks from the campfire
Are imitating the stars

They dance around us
As we hide amongst the pines

Creating constellations in your eyes

Intertwined with you
This is my universe

Strip down my soul
my Love
For it is craving your touch

Catch me if you can, my dear
And if you do
I hope you choose to run with me

— running with the wolves

I've learned that the bad stories
Are the hardest
Yet the best to tell

For wisdom leaks through their bindings

Oh, the sweet feeling
Of returning

It's almost as satisfying
As the Leave

For I come back a little different
Each time

Another night alone…

I can't help but wonder
If you're dreaming of me, too

Wherever we are in the world
Honey
When I'm with you
I have a sense of home

And still the guilt remains

I can feel its breath
On the back of my neck

Always lurking in the shadows
Waiting for the sun to sink

Just so it can wrap its arms around me
At night

They didn't believe me
When I told them what you did

Maybe they'd understand
If they could see

How I wake up in terror
In the middle of the night
As what happened is on replay
Like an endless role of film in my dreams

Or the images I can't erase
Every time I shut my eyes
Like they are plastered to the walls of my brain

Or hear the words you said play on repeat
Like a broken record throughout the days that I've bared since

        "only a little longer"
                "you can leave when I'm finished"

They don't believe me

But maybe they will if they could see
That the nightmare
That was my reality

Haunts me every day

Inflicting pain

Because I am terrified

Of feeling nothing at all

Baby Girl

It is not your fault

Saying no
Should've been enough
To stop him

Don't blame yourself
For something you could not control

Don't let his demons haunt you

Don't forget to find joy in simplicity

Put on your favorite playlist
And dance to the music
As you cook for one

Go for a stroll with yourself
Find a little coffee shop
Sit and read a while

Being alone
Doesn't mean you have to feel lonely

I used to mourn for people who were alone

Now I mourn for those who do not experience loneliness
At least once

The time to find You

You cannot run forever

There will come a time
When you finally have to face your demons...

Make sure you give them hell

I remember when
You came to me

You laid your worries at my feet
Gave up every burden you had

You let me fix them with
My words
My time
My thoughts
My soul

I sacrificed my own happiness
To assure that you had yours

I made myself soft
Allowed myself to feel again
Because I wanted to experience
All that you were

I let you in
Showed you every corner of my mind
And every inch of my skin

You wrecked them both
Then abandoned me with only your self-doubts
And now my own

I remember when
Your love was stronger than your pride

But now I'm left bare
Unmasked to the elements of
A broken heart

You came to me
And now I wish you never did

If love is blinding,
What is heartbreak?

You kissed me goodbye
And in my heart I knew
That it meant forever

Honey for you do not belong to me
She is the one who gets to love you out loud

I am the one in the shadows
Just begging you to stay

I had always known that I shouldn't fall for you
But now it's too late
I'm too far gone

So take your smile
And your laugh
And your memory
As you go

Because I cannot carry the weight
Of how you left my soul

And I can't explain it
How my heart longs for someone
I've yet to meet

Or places
That I've yet to see

You ask me what I'm thinking
When I stare out the window

And I can see in your eyes
That you want me to say you
And our life together

So the words spill out of me
Although I can tell
That my heart isn't present

Why am I so quick to guard your feelings
And to disregard my own?

Your eyes on me
That's all I care to wear

The idea of me
Having what we had
With someone else

I hope it makes you Cringe

All that I ask of you
Is to please be easy with my soul

For each given day
Is another opportunity
To do something absolutely profound

There is just something about
Whiskey, Campfires, and You

Take your dreams
And give them wings

Darling

Please look into yourself and see
That you are not just a flickering light

You are a blazing wildfire

Capable of engulfing the entire world
In your flames

Why does society tell us
    It is essential to seduce others
        With our appearance

Rather than to captivate them

    With our minds

Do not cower behind a made-up face
It does not do your soul enough justice

With high hopes
We are dreaming of better days

Too many believe
That they should cut off their emotions
Just so they do not have to hurt again

I am here to tell you,
Embrace everything you are

For your heart is far too warm
And you are too full of life
To be so cold

And scared to love

And on some nights
I long to feel you pull me into you
With a sleepy kiss placed on my spine
As you run your gentle fingers through
My messy hair

Some nights I long to be
Tangled up with you

I will not stop until
I feel absolute Bliss

The older I get
The more I understand

How essential
Adventure is for your soul

And I vow to spend my days
Wandering around cities that I feel lost in
To finally find comfort in myself

And despite it all
You'll learn to forgive yourself

CHEYENNE REID

She has a wandering heart
Planting roots in whatever soil she walks on

For this world has so much to give
And she has so much to offer

You can hold her
But you cannot hold her back

I roll over
And reach out for you
Just to feel frigid sheets
Crumble beneath my grasp

How do I adapt to an empty bed
When the presence of you
Still lingers within me?

Everything you've said
I still feel it all

All I want is
To become completely exposed

And not be ashamed
But to feel set free

Something so organic
It brings the life back into me
That I didn't know was missing

Someone so genuine

That the taste of honey
Has nothing on the sweetness
Of their lips on mine

All I want is to be accepted

In my Rawest form

I know what it's like
To escape something awful
Just to be trapped
In the same situation
With someone else

Do not let this discourage you
Not all love goes bad

Life is a beautiful chaos
That we can't help but dance in

And then on some nights
I get caught up in the oceans between us

The riptide of your memory takes me under without warning
Releases me long enough to come up for air

You keep me alive
Just to drag me back down again

You come and go in waves

When I love
I fall all in

And when I get burnt

I catch fire

I need something that is down to the bone
So deep that I feel you when you're a world away

To be alone and not feel lonely

A me and you
For eternity

And finally
>   I began to care for myself
>   The way I used to care about you

Oh, how sweet it is
To find love
After you fall for
Yourself first

It was 7 A.M.
With messy hair and oversized sweater
There was a slight chill in the air
As the scent of freshly brewed coffee
Inhabited my apartment

Curled up on the sofa
With my favorite novel
As I listened to the distant sound of the train
Roll seamlessly across the tracks

I gazed out into the fog-covered trees
And realized that in this moment

I was content with being alone

—When I discovered that I didn't need you

I've decided to be my own lighthouse

No matter how far my heart will stray
I will always return

For I have made a home in myself

Memories have a way of taking over me

Constantly replaying the moments
You altered my heart
To fit you oh so perfectly

How you'd grab my face
And kiss my lips so sweetly
Sealed with a blushing grin
As you pulled me into your chest

The open and vulnerable conversations
Shared on bar stools and in bed sheets

It seemed as if our foundation
Was built on whiskey and a melody
What a damn beautiful combination
Just as you and I

Now I cling onto these
Precious moments in time
Because that's all that I have left of you

And I'm not ready to let go of it all just yet

I'm not asking for your heart
My Dear

I'm only asking for
Some time
Some laughter
Some crazy
With you

But please
Do not give me your heart
Because I don't think I'm capable
Of caring for it
As well as I can
Your body and mind

You noticed her
As you scanned the hazy room

The way she could sway slow
To an upbeat tune

How she was perfectly comfortable in her skin
No matter the opinion of those watching

The smoke rolled from between her teeth
You wondered what she must be thinking of

She threw her head back
Eyes closed with the faintest grin

Oh, how she wore those neon lights so well

You wanted to go to her
To take her hand

But she doesn't need you
To feel this good

She's content with who she is
With or without you

You run your fingers
Down the ridges of my spine

Your eyes gently analyze
My exposed body

Your lips dance across my delicate skin;
Undressing me has become your favorite hobby

Oh, my Love
You so artfully have a way with my frame
But I can see that
When it comes to my mind, my spirit
You cannot comprehend the meaning

For I am more than these bones
That wrap around yours so perfectly

I am more than the soft moans
That are drawn out of me by your touch

This frame holds
A beautifully tender composition
Made up of a past and present
And a future that is still unwritten

How I wish you could realize
That I am more than this enthralling intimacy
We have created

Amongst the rooftops
Beneath the stars
Smoke from my cigarette
Burns my lungs

I look down at the chaos below
And wonder who
In this very moment
Feels as lonely as I do

I wonder who else is
Holding on to that inevitable hope
That we may find each other
Some day

I can't help but feel that you're out there

That you'll make all of this worth the wait

And then I felt it;

My heart still in my chest
After I had been so certain
That you took it with you when you left

When you begin to feel
As if every day is the same

And you grow tired of
The known

I encourage you to
Start each sun rising
As if it could be your last

Nourish the souls surrounding you
With unconditional love
And uncontrollable laughter

And if you have the chance
To take a chance
I hope you choose to take it

We are given this one life
This wonderful window of opportunity
To be whoever we desire to be

We say the biggest fear of man
Is failure
But don't we already fail
If we don't ever try?

I would rather take on days of
Heartbreak and loneliness
To truly discover myself

Than to be falsely loved
For my masks

And as I watched the sun
Kiss the sea goodnight

I hoped your toes were sunk
In the sand of a distant coast

I hoped that you felt the
Warmth rise above the waves

As if the light left me
Just to find you

Oh, my love
I hoped that you were
Thinking of me, too

May these hardships help you become
A light in the darkness
For the ones who are not strong enough
To hold their own flame

www.ingramcontent.com/pod-product-compliance
Lightning Source LLC
Chambersburg PA
CBHW060453080526
44584CB00015B/1418